OnBoard
ACADEMICS

I0083344

Prefixes and Suffixes

© 2015 OnBoard Academics, Inc
Portsmouth, NH
800-596-3175
www.onboardacademics.com
ISBN: 978-1-63096-029-2

ALL RIGHTS RESERVED. This book contains material protected under International and Federal Copyright Laws and Treaties. Any unauthorized reprint or use of this material is prohibited. No part of this book may be reproduced or transmitted in any form or by any means, electronic or mechanical, including photocopying, reprinting, recording, or by any information storage and retrieval system without expressed written permission from the author / publisher.

OnBoard Academic's books are specifically designed to be used as printed workbooks or as on-screen instruction. Each page offers focused exercises and students quickly master topics with enough proficiency to move on to the next level.

OnBoard Academic's lessons are used in over 25,000 classrooms to rave reviews. Our lessons are aligned to the most recent governmental standards and are updated from time to time as standards change. Correlation documents are located on our website. Our lessons are created, edited and evaluated by educators to ensure top quality and real life success.

Interactive lessons for digital whiteboards, mobile devices, and PCs are available at www.onboardacademics.com. These interactive lessons make great additions to our books.

You can always reach us at customerservice@onboardacademics.com.

Suffixes

Key Vocabulary

Suffix

Use the letter groups below to complete the sentences.

> These letter groups are called suffixes. When a suffix is added to the end of a root word, it creates a new word with a new definition.

Is that stray dog home_____ ?

Did your teach_____ give you a quiz today?

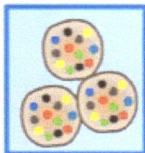

A recipe is help_____ when baking cookies.

| er | ful | less |

Suffixes

Write the new word in the box provided. Read the definition for the new word. How is the definition different from the root word?

root word		suffix		new word	definition
fast	+	est	=		the most fast
help	+	ful	=		full of help
care	+	less	=		without care

Complete the suffix chart.
Use the suggestions next to the chart to complete the suffix chart.

suffix	meaning
ful	
	similar/in this way
	state or quality of
ing	
	one who; more
est	

Word list (left of chart): Tasteful, Smoothly, Sadness, Cooking, Dependable, Painter, Careless, Biggest

Suggestion tiles:
- ly
- less
- er
- able
- ness
- happening now
- full of
- most
- without
- ability

Identify the suffix.
Read the definition and then draw a line from the root word to the correct suffix.
Write the new words in the space at the bottom.

est	brush	Brush now
ful	friend	Act like a friend
ness	tall	The most tall
er	thought	Full of thought
ing	soft	The stat of being soft
ly	teach	One who teaches

Sort the words to identify the correct suffix.
Sort the words by listing them in the correct suffix or incorrect suffix columns. For the words with incorrect suffixes, select one of the suffixes provided as a replacement suffix.

correct suffix	incorrect	suffix

joyest   kindly   lightest

safeable   washer   touchless

ing   ly   ful

Sometimes spelling changes when adding a suffix.
Study the illustration below to understand how to change spelling when adding a suffix in these instances.

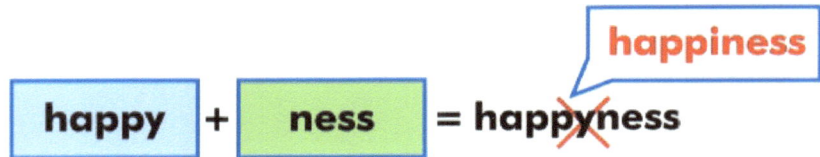

happiness

happy + ness = happyness (✗)

When adding a suffix to words ending in -y, the last letter is changed to -i.

cutest

cute + est = cuteest (✗)

Words ending with a silent -e drop the letter before a suffix *beginning with a vowel*.

---

1 relyable ☐

2 safest ☐

3 glideing ☐

4 noteable ☐

5 pityful ☐

6 prettiest ☐

Mark the correctly spelled words with a check mark and the incorrectly spelled words with an X.

Complete the sentences using the correct suffix.

Alison usual_____ eats breakfast at school.

Mia was breath_____ after the 100 yard dash.

James tried to make himself comfort_____ .

Tori is a great sing_____ .

Grace has the soft_____ blanket.

| able | ly | est | less | er |

Name_____

Suffix Quiz

1. True or false? A suffix is added at the beginning of a word.

2. Circle the letter group that is not a suffix. ly less dis ing

3. Circle the suffix changes the word listen to mean one who listens. ing er able est

4. Fill in the blank. That was the great _____ song I ever heard !

5. Fill in the blank. It is cold_____ in the winter than in the summer. ing er able ness

6. Fill in the blank. The bell was ring_____ loudly. ing er able est

7. Fill in the blank. The directions were help_____ to us. ly ness able ful

8. Add the suffix ful to beauty. _____.

©2013 OnBoard Academics, Inc.   www.onboardacademics.com

Suffixes and Spelling

Key Vocabulary

Suffix

CVC word

CCVC word

Sometimes adding a **suffix** can change the **spelling** of the root word.

Put an X in the circle when you identify the difference. Put a check mark in the circle if there is no difference.

stop

s t o p p e d

excite

e x c i t e d

study

s t u d i e d

Are the root word and the suffix combination correct?

CVC=Consonant Vowel Consonant
CCVC=Consonant Consonant Vowel Consonant

> When adding the suffix -ed or -ing to a CVC or CCVC word, the final consonant of the root word needs to be doubled.

cutting

cut + ing = cuting

flipped

flip + ed = fliped

Build the missing words.

Use the colored boxes at the bottom to build your answers.

James _____ his foot to the beat.

The cat _____ at the ball of yarn.

I was _____ at the end of the play.

Grace was _____ with Jenna.

| bat | chat | clap | tap | ed | ing | p | t |

When adding a suffix beginning with a **vowel** to a word ending with **-e**, the final **-e** of the root word is dropped.

care + **ed** = c~~are~~ed → **cared**

live + **ing** = liv~~e~~ing → **living**

Sort the words.

correct spelling	incorrect spelling

createed   caring   exciting

blameed   wasteing   placed

_____

> When adding **-ed** or **-es** to a word ending with **-y**, drop the -y and add an **-i** to the root word.

carried

carry + ed = ca~~rry~~ed

stories

story + es = sto~~ry~~es

Add the suffix to make a new word.

carry + ed = _____

story + es = _____

sky + es = _____

party + es = _____

apply + ed = _____

puppy + es = _____

Identify the sentence with the correct spelling by putting a check mark in the box.

1	Owen has traveled to ten cityes.	☐
2	My mom dropped me off at school	☐
3	The woman siped her soda.	☐
4	David hurried to his desk.	☐
5	My sister likeed her new toy.	☐
6	The dog was siting on the floor.	☐

Name_____

Suffixes and Spelling Quiz
Circle the correct answer.

1. The correct plural of pony is ponyes. True or false.

2. The boy was _____ to first base.
   runing   running   runnning   runeing

3. I _____ my wish would come true.
   hopped   hopes   hoped   hooped

4. We were _____ the soccer ball.
   chaseing   chasing   chaysing   chaseng

5. The coach _____ his hands.
    waving   waveing   waved   wavd

6. We _____ for the team.
   claped   clapped   clapping   claping

7. It was an _____ game!
   exciteing   excited   excitd   exciting

8. I found three _____ on the floor.
   pennys   pennyes   pennies   penny

©2013OnBoard Academics, Inc.

Prefixes

Key vocabulary

Prefix

Root word

Prefixes

Study the illustration below to learn about prefixes.

> A prefix is a group of letters that appears before a root word and changes the root word's meaning.

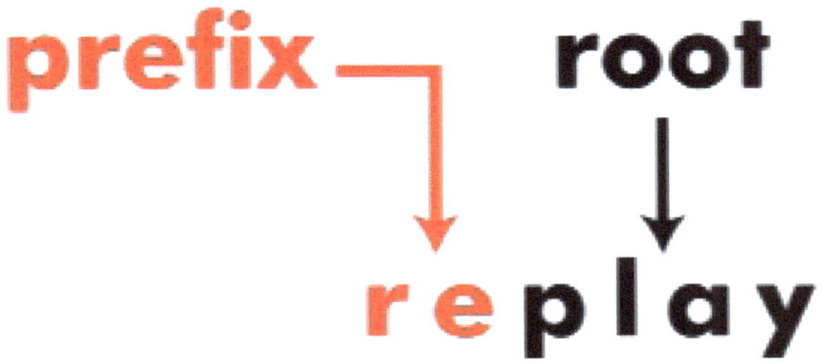

prefix ──┐   **root**
             │   ↓
             ↓
          re p l a y

re + play = replay

What do these prefixes mean?
Select a prefix for each root word that matches the definition.

un	pre	re	mis

____soak   =   soak **before**

____paint   =   paint **again**

____safe   =   **not** safe

____match   =   **wrong** match

Match the prefix to the correct meaning.
Write the prefix in the correct box.

unhappy   [   ] = before

rebuild   [   ] = three

pretest   [   ] = not

misspell   [   ] = again

triangle   [   ] = under

subway   [   ] = wrong

Match the root words with a prefix to make a new word by writing it under the correct prefix.

un	pre	mis

behave	lock	view

heat	trust	usual

©2013 OnBoard Academics, Inc.

Use the correct prefix from the list below to complete this passage.

Alison and her family went to the movies over the weekend. Her mom _____placed the car keys, so they had to take the _____way. They were _____able to make it in time for the first showing, so they _____paid for the late show to make sure they got in. It was almost midnight when they _____turned to their house!

| un | sub | mis | re | pre |

How do you know if a word really does have a prefix?

uncle

unhappy

Remove the letters that you think form a prefix, and if you're left with a root word, then you know that the original word probably *does* have a prefix.

The word "uncle" does not have a prefix, but the word "unhappy" does.

_____

Which of these words has a prefix?

Place √ if the word has a prefix and an X if it does not.

1	uncover	
2	pretty	
3	submarine	
4	misunderstand	
5	ready	
6	prehistoric	

Name_____

Prefix Quiz

1. A prefix is added at the beginning of the word. Circle answer True or False

2. Circle the prefix. pre ment tion able

3. Which of the following words does not have a prefix? uncover redo triple miscalculated.

4. Fill in the blank. Be sure to _____ read the page to make sure you understand the main idea. un re pre mis

5. Fill in the blank. My white and blue socks were a _____ match. un re pre mis

6. Fill in the blank. You need to _____ zip your coat before you take it off. un re pre mis

7. Fill in the blank.   We had to _____ heat the oven to warm it up. un   re pre mis

8. When the prefix "pre" is added to the root word "game", what is the meaning of the new word. Put a check mark next to the correct answer.
   a. play the game again
   b. before the game
   c. after the game
   d. bad game

Prefixes and Suffixes

Key Vocabulary

prefix

suffix

root word

Prefix

Add a single prefix to all of the blanks in the passage.

> A prefix is a group of letters that
> appears before a root word and
> changes the root word's meaning.

Some people think pro football players are

_____ rated and _____ paid.

But imagine if your quarterback makes a

a big play in _____ time, or a wide

receiver makes a great _____ head catch.

You'd be _____ joyed!

What does prefix mean? _____

Prefix

Match the prefix with its meaning.

unhappy

rebuild

pretest

misspell

triangle

subway

pre	= before
	= three
	= not
	= again
	= under
	= wrong

Add prefixes to make new words.

prefix	+	root	=	new word	meaning
	+	state	=	?	exaggerate
	+	state	=	?	say again
	+	state	=	?	call something too low
	+	state	=	?	speak in error

re	mis	under	over

How do you know if a word has a prefix or not?

uncle

unhappy

Remove the letters that you think form a prefix, and if you're left with a root word, then you know that the original word probably does have a prefix.

The word "uncle" does not have a prefix, but the word "unhappy" does.

Which word has a prefix?
Place a √ if it has a prefix and an X if it doesn't.

Hide the 'prefix' to see if it leaves a root word

1	uncover	
2	pretty	
3	submarine	
4	misunderstand	
5	ready	
6	prehistoric	

©2013 OnBoard Academics, Inc.   www.onboardacademics.com

Suffix

> A suffix is a group of letters that when added to the end of a root word, changes the root word's meaning, and/or its part of speech. It's possible to have more than one suffix on the end of a root word, e.g. play (verb), play-ful (adj.), and playfulness (noun).

Connect the suffix to the root word.

brush	est
friend	ful
tall	ness
thought	er
soft	ing
teach	ly

©2013 OnBoard Academics, Inc.   www.onboardacademics.com

Spelling with Suffixes
The silent e

> Keep the silent e when adding a consonant suffix. Drop the silent e when adding a vowel suffix, including a y *vowel* suffix.

Complete the new word while being careful of spelling.

root + suffix = new word

taste	+	ful	=	
taste	+	y	=	
taste	+	ing	=	

| tastful | tasty | tastey |
| tasteing | tasteful | tasting |

©2013 OnBoard Academics, Inc.   www.onboardacademics.com

Root words ending in -ce or -ge and teh -able and -ous suffixes

For root words ending in -ce or -ge,
keep the e if the suffix is -able or -ous.

enforce + able = enforceable

outrage + ous = outrageous

Suffixes and Spelling-Words Ending in -y

Complete the new word.

word + suffix = new word

play	+	ful	=	

busy	+	ly	=	

worry	+	ing	=	

plaiful	busyly	worriing
worrying	playful	busily

©2013 OnBoard Academics, Inc.   www.onboardacademics.com

Repeating the Final Consonant

C V C	**consonant-vowel-consonant**
V V C	**vowel-vowel-consonant**

In one-syllable CVC words, *usually* double the final consonant if the suffix begins with a vowel.

C V C

ship	shipping
	shipper
	shipped
	shipment

V V C

cool	cooling
	cooler
	cooled
	coolness

©2013 OnBoard Academics, Inc.　　　www.onboardacademics.com

Name_____

Prefixes and Suffixes Quiz

1. If you add the suffix -ing to the word float, you need to double the last consonant. True or false?

2. Which word is not spelled correctly?
   a. pityful
   b. peaceful
   c. playful
   d. wonderful

3. What is the meaning of the prefix sub?
   a. above, on top of, beyond
   b. below, secondary
   c. not, opposite of
   d. again, back

4. Which word is correctly spelled?
   a. makeing
   b. making
   c. mackeing
   d. makking
   e.

5. Enforce plus the suffix able is spelled enforcable. True or false?

www.ingramcontent.com/pod-product-compliance
Lightning Source LLC
Chambersburg PA
CBHW060815090426
42737CB00002B/73